MW00638188

Why People Live in New Orleans

Why People Live in New Orleans

Gene, as a fellow educator, I am thrilled to imagine the people you serve getting to know our city better because of your visit to New Orleans. May all your memories be good ones, and may you return often for more! Thanks for coming!

Christine Allen Ewy

Christine Allen Ewy

June 16, 2010

Calereka Books
Metairie, Louisiana

Copyright © 2009 by Christine Allen Ewy
All rights reserved.

This work may not be reproduced, in whole or in part, (beyond that permitted by Sections 107 and 108 of the U.S. Copyright Law and except for reviews) without prior written permission from the author.

www.christineallenewy.com

Published by Calereka Books
1937 Veterans Blvd. PMB 339
Metairie, Louisiana 70005
Calereka@cox.net

Printed in Hong Kong

Ewy, Christine Allen
   Why people live in New Orleans
   x, 96 cm.
   Includes bibliographical references and index.
   ISBN 978-0-615-29934-1 (hardcover)
   1. New Orleans (La.)—National importance. 2. New Orleans (La.)—History. 3. New Orleans (La.)—Social characteristics and culture. 4. New Orleans (La.)—Environmental concerns. 5. Community life—New Orleans (La.). 6. Community action—New Orleans (La.)

Cover photograph by Dominic Koric

Dedicated to Michael Allen

Fly free you sandy-haired sailor

May the wind fill your spirit sail wide

May the oceans you see on your journeys

Always greet you with sparkling eyes.

Fly free you kind, gentle sailor

May your lighthearted gestures live long.

We'll keep memories of your childlike style

And always remember your sunshine water smile.

Fly free with love and light,

Flow with the river of your soul.

Katrina Ariel Koric

About the Author

New Orleans is my birthplace and home of choice. My early years were spent in the Lower Garden District, in what were the St. Thomas Projects and nearby neighborhoods, where I learned a love of urban New Orleans—the ability to walk to the store, school, and movie theater, or to hop on the streetcar or bus for more. I was also grateful for the companionship of neighbors, especially in the evening after the busyness of the day yielded to being outside in the cooler air and visiting. We had little at the time, and I was grateful for community resources, such as the ones Kingsley House offered and still does today.

We had family who lived in other parts of the city, such as elders who lived a couple of blocks off St. Charles, where we used to spend Mardi Gras each year. The beauty of the trees and architecture thrilled me as we walked or rode the streetcar in the Garden District, Uptown, to Audubon Park, and to Canal Street. As a carpenter, my dad had built or repaired many houses in those areas as well as the rest of the city, so when we got a car he would introduce me to the many neighborhoods, and my appreciation of the city, its architecture, and its culture deepened.

My uncles were in the merchant marines, so they'd take me to their ships docked at the wharf, where the river got in my blood. When we moved to Metairie, we were about eight blocks from the lake, and that body of water became the center of many activities, only to be treasured more when I pursued my undergraduate degree at the University of New Orleans on the lakefront. During my teens and college, I learned about the areas of Bucktown, West End, Lakeview, City Park, Gentilly, and the French Quarter.

I often went to the Quarter to study and walk after classes. I also volunteered as an informal tour guide for international visitors, and thus had a reason to learn more about the city myself.

These personal experiences—plus visiting friends, relatives, and community resources in other parts of the area—gave me a love of greater New Orleans in its entirety, rather than one localized neighborhood. It is this love of the whole that brought me back after work took me away for a number of years.

After Hurricanes Katrina and Rita, each time I heard out-of-state friends, news media, congressmen, and citizens around the world ask, "Why do people live in New Orleans?" I felt a need for a resource to specifically answer their question. That is the reason I wrote *Why People Live in New Orleans*.

My vita is posted on my web site:

www.christineallenewy.com

Contact Information:
1937 Veterans Blvd. PMB 339
Metairie, Louisiana 70005
caebks8@cox.ner

Contents

Acknowledgments

"Why do people live in New Orleans?," the question prompting this book, required a response from a diverse group of people representing the area. I am, therefore, grateful to the many residents who willingly helped form that response, and to our culture that enabled me to stop people on the street, in the park, at cafés, and all around town to ask their thoughts. Some interviews were prearranged, and Pushpa Ramiaiah, Youth Services Program Manager at Kingsley House, and Carole Mundt, Assistant Principal at Chalmette High School, were very kind to connect me with youth and adults in their areas of the city.

Gracious experts took time from their busy schedules to provide, verify, or clarify many facts and to offer resources for the pragmatic answer to why people live in New Orleans. My humble gratitude to Pat Borne, Jefferson Parish Public Information Officer; Maria Cervini, Executive Assistant, Jefferson Parish Drainage Department; Katherine Costanza, Assistant Director, Jefferson Parish Department of Environmental Affairs; Greg DuCote, LA State Contact for the Gulf of Mexico Community Based Restoration Partnership; Carlton Dufrechou, Executive Director of the Lake Pontchartrain Basin Foundation; Wade J. Habshey, Public Affairs Officer, Task Force Hope; Sara-Ann Harris, Communications Director, Louisiana Seafood Board; Clifford Hearn, Center for Coastal and Watershed Studies, USGS, St. Petersburg, Florida; Don Hinrichsen and John Rowley, People and Planet, Planet 21; George Paul Kemp, Vice-President for the Gulf Coast Initiative of the National Audubon Society; John A. Lopez, Director, Coastal Sustainability Program, Lake Pontchartrain Basin Foundation; Fabrizio Maronta, Limes-Rivista Italiana di Geopolitica; Bob Pavlik, Assistant Director, Institute for the Transformation of Learning, Marquette University; Paul Pickering, Shell Oil Company; Susan Testroet-Bergeron, Barataria-Terrebonne National Estuary Program; and James Wilkins, Louisiana Sea Grant Law and Policy Program.

Any writer who wants to produce a quality product needs a third group of people during the writing process. I thank these reviewers who read one or more drafts of the work and provided their thoughtful feedback. From the New Orleans area: Jackie Graff, Licensed New Orleans Tour Guide; Lea Sinclair, Director of Communications, N.O. Tourism Marketing Corporation; Michael Weil, Jewish Federation of Greater New Orleans; and residents Claire Bergeron, Wilfredo and Rose Escalante, Anthony and Yvonne Hymel, and Mignon and Mark Swinney. From outside the region: Filippa Graziano from Australia; Dave King from California; Kristina Hesbol, Art and Carol Rush, and Linda Vass from Illinois; Bob Rhodes from Virginia; Nate Leishman, LDS Humanitarian Services, Manager, Emergency Response, Utah.

My thanks to our talented daughter, Katrina Ariel Koric, for her poetic dedication to my brother, Michael Allen, as well as her artistic and technological skills with book layout, photograph quality enhancement, and design of my web site. Molly Ebert was also a world of help, refining our work to make it printer-ready, and gently teaching me much along the way.

Hugs to encouraging friends, such as Jerri Hebert, who pitched in at one of my book expos. Also, unending gratitude to my husband, Bob Ewy. He frequently served as taxi driver for my research and photography, porter at my book exhibits, reviewer in spite of the countless times I asked his opinion, patient companion when out with me and I disappeared to do a spontaneous interview, subject of some of the photographs, and champion along the way.

Photograph Credits

Linda Balfour
   Page 12 as noted

Christine Allen Ewy
   All photos not otherwise acknowledged

David King
   Pages 2 bottom right, 56 "Dr. Saxtrum"

Dominic Koric
   Cover, pages 5 City Park tree, 25 streetcar, 31 all but two at bottom right, 55 left, 56 top right, 65 bottom center and right

Patsy Lynch/FEMA
   Page 14 as noted

Tony Martin
   Pages 35, 46 top center, 55 bottom

Marvin Newman/FEMA
   Page 14 as noted

The Times Picayune
   Page 12 as noted

U.S. Army Corps of Engineers
   Page 14 as noted

Map Credits

Army Corps of Engineers
   Greater N.O. map pages 3, 17, 28, and 29

Barataria-Terrebonne National Estuary Program
   Land loss maps page 37

CIA's *The World Fact Book*
   The Netherlands page 44

Heartland Asian Review of Geopolitics
   World map with N.O. strategic location pages 2 and 8

National Atlas of the United States
   Louisiana map page 38

National Park Service
   Mississippi River U.S. watershed pages 9 and 10

Wikipedia
   Louisiana and U.S. maps page 3

x

Some people have wondered . . .

Why do people live in the New Orleans area?

There are several ways to answer the question:

I can tell you the practical reasons why New Orleans needs to exist and why people need to live here for the nation's and world's best interests, if I interpret the question as, "Why would anyone live in an area where environmental challenges are presenting themselves to the world with increasing urgency?" Practical reasons use facts to logically replace misconceptions and speak to fears and frustrations.

I can also tell you the reasons that are compelling to residents, including my family, giving you our points of view to answer the question's other interpretation, "Why do current residents live here, knowing these challenges?" This approach offers the thoughts, feelings, and facts of people's lives that we weigh against the risks.

A third question lurking near these two is, "What impacts do the unfolding events in the New Orleans area have on me and people living in the rest of the world?"

Given the reality that more than half the world and half the U.S. populations live, like Orleanians and their neighbors, within fifty miles of coasts, we need all of the above to fully understand the factors that our area's challenges foreshadow for the world.[1] With such understanding, we can act upon the stake we all have in this area and its regeneration, and do so in a way that adds to our ability to sustain and regenerate the rest of the world.

This book can be an easy tool for discussing and answering the question(s), exploring related issues and possible solutions, and strengthening our ability to make informed decisions and take positive actions.

1

Why would anyone live in the New Orleans area?

The nation and the world need stewards of the area's abundant natural resources, strategic location, and de facto center for studying and acting upon urgent environmental and social changes affecting the world. The following pages illustrate and invoke this **interdependence.**

Why do current residents live here?

We cherish *the* place, *our* place, *the* people, and *our* people here, **and** we know that **the resulting lifestyle and culture could not be recreated or transported elsewhere.**

We are known for enthusiastically welcoming visitors to share this lifestyle and culture. Other residents and I do so again through these pages, as we relate our compelling reasons for carefully weighing and repeatedly accepting the risks of stewardship of this area we call home.

Mom eating a" snowball"
Magazine Street,
New Orleans ~ 1940

My parents, brother, and I
Irish Channel , New Orleans ~ 1951

Multiple generations of our family
Metairie ~ 1959

My husband and I
French Quarter,
New Orleans ~ 2006

The Place — Location

The area's vast natural resources and strategic location provide the beauty, diversity–and, of course, challenges—of a world port nearly surrounded by water in a subtropical climate.

Courtesy of Wikipedia

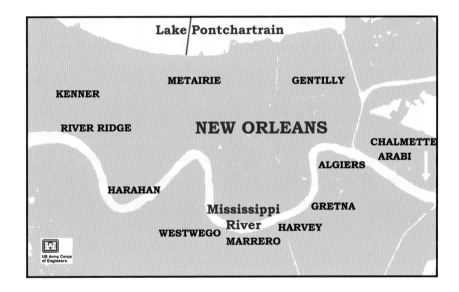

Location — Coastal Proximity

Peter Weber, in "It Comes Down to the Coasts," explains, "Though they are the most vulnerable of Earth's ecosystems, the coasts house biological processes and diversity that are essential to the health and stability of the biosphere as a whole."

He elaborates with this list of benefits of coastal areas that have wetlands and estuaries:[2]

- Scenic beauty

- Fertile soil and coastal waters

- Essential fish and wildlife habitat

- Wetland filtering of some pollutants out of runoff water, slowing the speed of runoff, reduction of erosion, and buffering of storm surges from hurricanes and tropical storms

- Many products, including medicines, derived from the soils and plants

- International trade

- Tourism

- Multiple forms of recreation

- Jobs supporting all of the above

People *outside* the coastal zones have wanted people to live *in* them if they, too, were to benefit from these regions. Thus we see why among continents, only in Africa do more people live in the interior than along or near ocean coasts, but even in Africa demographics are shifting.[3]

People in the New Orleans area, with their coastal neighbors, have enjoyed and provided national and global access to the abundant benefits of the Gulf of Mexico. The ninth-largest body of water in the world,[4] the Gulf of Mexico houses 40% of the nation's most productive of all ecosystems—wetlands and estuaries—where rivers turn brackish as they enter the sea.[5]

Great Outdoors!

Our subtropical climate and natural resources allow us to walk our dog year-round in our neighborhood, in parks, and by scenic waterways—the lake, river, or bayou. We love the beautiful live oak trees. Some are over 600 years old! As a youth I loved to climb them; lots of people still do.

"I came here because it was warm like India, where I'm from. New Orleans needs doctors, so business has been good. Now that I've done well, I would feel a bit guilty leaving the people who need me."

~ Dr. Kiran Zaveri

City Park lost over 1,000 trees from flooding after Hurricane Katrina, but fortunately, many survived.

Audubon Park

Michael Villafranco at City Park

"This area has a lot of natural beauty, such as the native swamps and the Gulf."

~ Lily

Lily Moret

"I like the big trees. The parks are fun 'cause I meet all kinds of kids from different cities."

~ Jasmine

Jasmine Williams

"The warm weather makes it easier to go out in the fall and winter, and to go fishing with our dad."

~ Laura & Nick

Laura & Nick Youngblood

"It's a fun place to live. When you go to the park you start meeting new people and later you get to meet them over again."

~Autumn

Autumn Richards

"We like to play in the sun and splash in the water."

~ Jaron & Jason

Jaron & Jason Halley

"I like the **bayous, marshes, landscape,** and the **weather**—not too hot or too cold. We also have some of the best **fishing and hunting** in the nation."

~ S. Joseph Salvaggio

Location — Gulf of Mexico

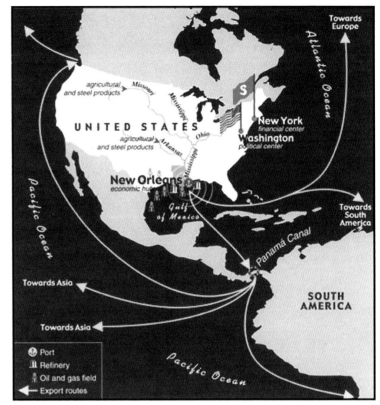

Courtesy of Heartland Eurasian Review of Geopolitics

Strategic Location

The United States and the world have needed people to live in the New Orleans area because of its larger role in **linking the interior of North America with the ocean** via the Mississippi River and its countless tributaries.[6] New Orleans' strategic location near the intersection of the mouth of the Mississippi and the Gulf of Mexico has made the area what political scientist George Friedman called "a geopolitical prize."

Some of the Gulf of Mexico's Resources

• Seven of the top ten U.S. seaports[8]

• Some of the most productive fisheries in the world; four of the top seven fishing ports in the nation by weight; more finfish, shrimp, and shellfish yield annually than the south and mid-Atlantic, Chesapeake, and New England areas combined; and productive recreational fishery[9]

• Called "America's Energy Coast," the Gulf of Mexico contributes more than 44% of the crude oil, 43% of the dry natural gas, and more than 50% of liquid natural gas that fuels this nation.[10]

• Habitat for numerous fish and wildlife species, including migrating waterfowl, seabirds, wading birds, and furbearers[11]

• The largest concentration of oceanographers engaged in science and research in the world—part of the Gulf of Mexico Program located at John C. Stennis Space Center in Mississippi, 45 miles east of New Orleans[12]

Strategic Location

Economic and Political Importance

- Archeological evidence referenced by John Folse in *The Encyclopedia of Cajun & Creole Cuisine* suggests Native Americans' trade economy in the area thrived as early as Ramses II, Moses, and the Phoenicians.[13]

- France and Spain each controlled the area for the economic purposes of trade, the established port, and navigation to the rest of the territory, as well as for the political purposes of preventing other countries' access to the river and further colonization.

- The United States bought it for similar reasons. In 1801 Spain ceded Louisiana back to France. With no access to the crucial port of New Orleans and the Mississippi River, Americans feared war with France. Peirce Lewis, in *New Orleans, the Making of an Urban Landscape*, credits Thomas Jefferson, then U.S. President, for recognizing the New Orleans area as **indispensable for America's well-being and a gate-keeper to the nation's interior.**[14]

New Orleans' **strategic location** has required people here to safeguard the interests of the nation and the world throughout history. The area and its people now have another **central role**: helping the world learn how to resolve urgent **environmental** needs impacting economics, politics, and daily life the world over.

Before buying *La Louisianne* (yellow area at right) from France, the United States consisted only of the land east of the Mississippi River, and the Americans had no legal use of the river.

Location — the river

This map shows part of the river system upon which our nation and the world have depended. This third-largest drainage basin in the world sends water from rain and snow of 31 states and two Canadian provinces into major local rivers.[15] Those rivers all flow into the Mississippi River. The Mississippi flows into the ports in and around New Orleans and on into the Gulf of Mexico.

The Mississippi River and Its United States Watershed

Redrawn from National Parks Service image

Some Mississippi River Benefits

- Water supply all along the river—15 millon people in the basin's upper half alone depend on the river and its tributaries for drinking water. No figures are available for the lower half.[16]

- Ports along the Mississippi handle 56% of the nation's grain shipments and the nation's top market share for import steel, natural rubber, plywood, and coffee.[17] Gulf Coast ports anticipate growth from increased Asian markets and expansion of the Panama Canal.

- The Port of New Orleans connects to 19,000 miles of inland waterways.[18] It is the only deep-water port in the United States served by six class-one railroads, providing direct-access rail service to anywhere in the country. There are also ocean carriers, barge lines, and truck lines.[19]

- The 52,000 port-related jobs are reasons for people to live here.[20] Shipbuilding, aerospace manufacturing, military operations, the cruise industry, tourism, and the petrochemical industry require more people.

- Including the oil and gas production in the Gulf of Mexico, Louisiana is the second leading natural-gas producer in the country and the third leading crude-oil producer. Crude-oil production and imports that are not sent to other states are processed at Louisiana's 19 operating refineries, clustered mostly along the Lower Mississippi River and in the Lake Charles area.[21] Twenty-seven percent of America's oil and 30% of its gas travels through Louisiana's coast, serving half of the nation's refinery capacity.[22]

The River — a source of residents' livelihood and pleasure

The river is an integral part of residents' lives. We locals say we are going "uptown" or "downtown" depending on our destination's relationship to the river's current. We also give directions using "on the river side," or "going towards or away from the river." Walking along or sitting by the river are enjoyable pastimes. Watching the river and its traffic—international ships, flat barges, little tugboats, the ferry, and even a remaining steamboat—can entertain some, including me, for a long time. Of course, we can also get on one of those vessels or enjoy the shops, theatre, aquarium, restaurants, and the French Quarter only a few feet away.

The River — an invitation to broader perspectives

Living in a major port city can create the desire to see the rest of the world. Some family members and I did so, then returned to this area. The global perspective strengthened the draw of our home town. We knew that upon our return we could continue to enjoy the diversity that we valued while traveling and living elsewhere.

Louis Whitlow

Chiefs Wilford Woods & Louis Whitlow

Photo © 2009 The Times-Picayune Publishing Co., all rights reserved. Used with permission of The Times-Picayune Publishing Co., all rights reserved.

Many Orleanians remember dancing on the steamboat *President* and listening to the calliope music when she was docked. After finishing a Merchant Marine career, my uncle, Louis Whitlow, became Chief Engineer on the *President*, which was the river's last side-wheeler. As of October 2008 the town of St. Elmo, Illinois, had bought the 300-foot-long, five-story vessel, with plans to turn it into an 80-room hotel, convention center, and museum.

Photo courtesy of Linda Balfour, granddaughter of long-time pilot Captain Kelly King

River challenges—Spillways help keep the Mississippi River from overflowing its banks in the New Orleans area. One instance was in April 2008. Heavy rains and flooding had occurred in the river's watershed in some Midwestern states north of Louisiana. When the river level got close to the flood stage of 17 feet in the New Orleans area, the Army Corps of Engineers opened this spillway, sending river water into Lake Pontchartrain for the first time in 11 years.

Mississippi River

Floodway to Lake

"needles"

Normally, 350 bays and 7,000 "needles," or creosote-treated timbers, hold back the river water. When the river gets too high, engineers raise these "needles" to open the spillway.[23]

River Challenges

We are among many around the world who are alert to weather forecasts and river conditions throughout the year.

My husband and I were caught in the 1976 flood of the Big Thompson River in the mountains of Colorado, the worst natural disaster in Colorado history.

That experience and floods around the world, including events shown on the right, remind us that rivers everywhere always have the potential to flood their banks.

Big Thompson Canyon, CO ~ 1976
Remains of our family's cabin after the flood

Kenner, Louisiana ~ February 2005
Photo by U.S. Army Corps of Engineers

Snohomish, WA ~ November 2006
Photo by Marvin Nauman / FEMA

Northwestern Missouri ~ May 2007
Photo by Patsy Lynch / FEMA

The Lake — another compelling reason for residents to live here

Lake Pontchartrain—Like our other waterways this lake is a source of livelihood and pleasure. It is the second-largest saltwater lake in the country, Utah's being the largest. Louisiana provides more crab, shrimp, oysters, and crawfish than any other state in the nation.[24] A lot of it comes from here in the New Orleans area. Locals often gather outdoors around tables covered with seafood and vegetables that were boiled together in a big pot with spices. My husband and I love these well-seasoned shellfish. We also think the shrimpers and fishermen help make the lake an interesting place to spend time, as do the pelicans and seagulls often waiting for them.

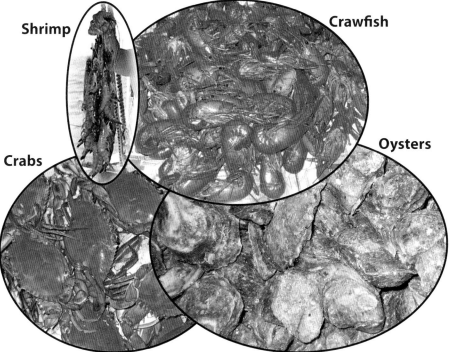

Shrimp

Crawfish

Crabs

Oysters

The lake, in fact, offers us a lot to do and see. We walk this path often. Runners and bicyclists like it, too. Other parts of the lake have steps along the shore going down into the water. All along the lakefront, people enjoy having picnics, flying kites, trying their luck with a fishing pole, or just taking in the beauty. Boaters, water skiers, and kite surfers entertain themselves and those watching. The pelicans, sea gulls, ducks, and occasional mullet jumping out of the water can be equally as fascinating. Our dog likes to chase waves.

Levees
These dirt hills were built after high lake water flooded Jefferson Parish in 1947.

Causeway
A 24-mile-long bridge across the lake

Lake Challenges

Most of Metairie (originally a French word about farming, now pronounced "Mettery" or "Metry") is between two and seven feet below sea level[25] and we get a lot of rain. That's why this pumping station near the walking path, and all the others in the greater New Orleans area, are very important to us. You see …

Metairie

Adapted from map by the Army Corps of Engineers

Lake Pontchartrain

KENNER

METAIRIE GENTILLY

RIVER RIDGE **NEW ORLEANS**

CHALMETTE
ARABI

ALGIERS

HARAHAN

Mississippi GRETNA
River HARVEY
WESTWEGO MARRERO

US Army Corps
of Engineers.

When rainwater builds up in city canals, the pumping station sends the water out to the lake. The station also normally keeps lake water from coming back in.[26]

We're looking at the 17th Street Canal, with the lake behind us. The canal separates New Orleans and Metairie. This was one origin of major flooding in 2005.

When Hurricane Katrina forced lake water back into the canal, it pushed down part of a wall on the New Orleans side that we've since found out was not built well. (You can see the rebuilt section of the wall on the left of the photo.) Water poured into Lakeview, other parts of New Orleans, and parts of Metairie farther south. Work continues on the canal.

New Orleans

Metairie

Engineers have also done considerable work at the lake end of the 17th Street Canal. They've built a gate to keep the lake water from coming back into the canal during future hurricanes, and they've installed more pumps to get rain water out when the gates are closed.

Gate seen from lake

Gate and pumps seen from canal

Remember the pumps we saw near the path?

We now have this "safe room" behind them. When Hurricane Katrina came, the people working the pumps were in danger, so they were ordered to leave and the pumps stopped.

That's a major reason why Metairie flooded.

Now pump operators are able to stay in the safe room to help prevent flooding from storms.

The **Place** — More reasons why residents cherish it

We'll return to practical reasons for our stewardship and concerns prompting the question of why people live here, but first let's broaden your knowledge of what we weigh against the risks:

The New Orleans area offers the essentials, attractions, and culture of a big city steeped in history; the convenience, informality, and heart of a small town; and the variety of multiple communities with their own appeal located near each other. (It only takes about fifteen minutes by car to go from the lake to the river, and about thirty to cross from east to west.)

Big City, Small Town

Attractions and history of a big city
This is the center of the French Quarter, where New Orleans began: Jackson Square sits in front of St. Louis Cathedral, which is flanked by two museums, the Cabildo and Presbytère. Filled with history, artists, shops, excellent restaurants, intriguing architecture, and frequent events, we never tire of this area.

Informality and heart of a small town
Each Christmas season, we join other residents and visitors for an evening of Christmas caroling. My enthusiasm starts to rise as we fill the square, entering from each of its four sides, carrying candles and songbooks. The friendly fun continues as we go on to sing, laugh, and enjoy this festive time together.

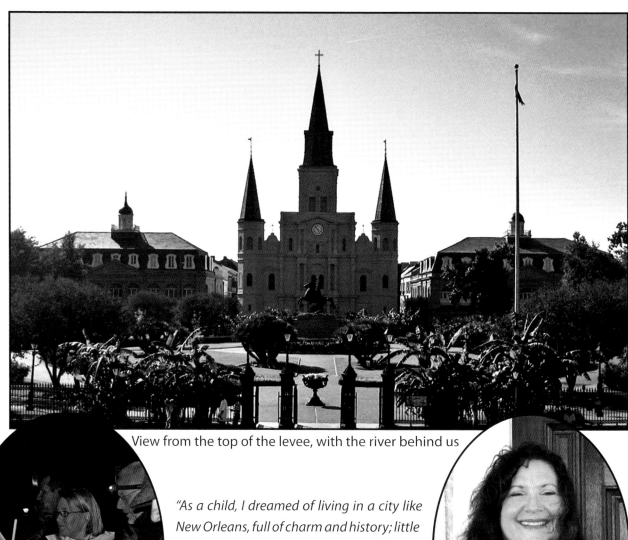

View from the top of the levee, with the river behind us

"As a child, I dreamed of living in a city like New Orleans, full of charm and history; little did I know I would meet and marry a New Orleanian. I love it here. Every time I enter the city, I feel like I'm a tourist on vacation."

~ Cheryl Bergeron

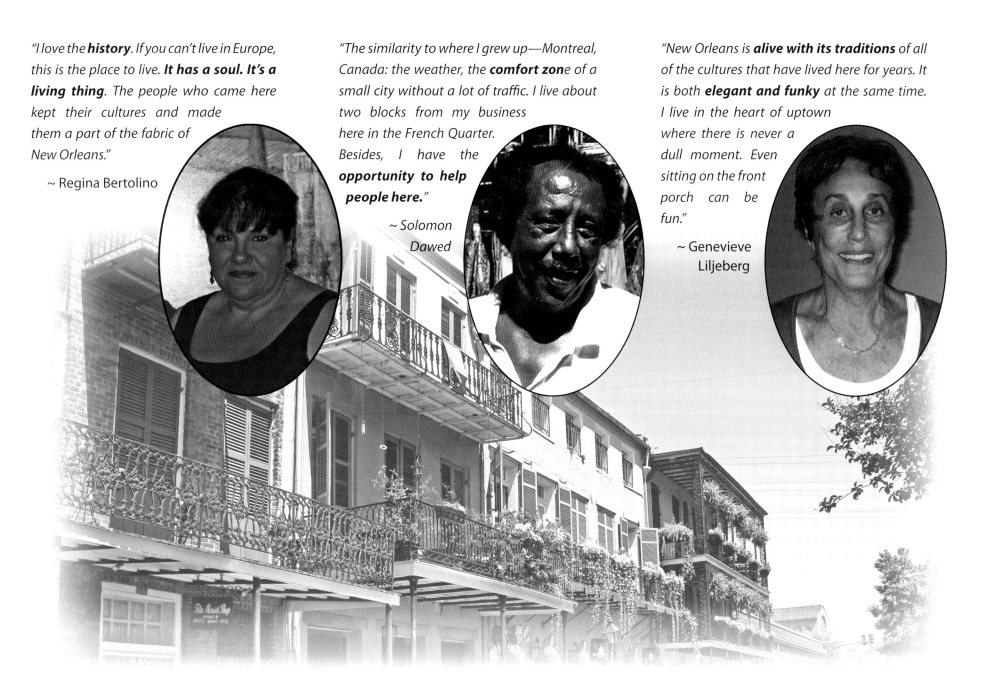

"I love the **history**. If you can't live in Europe, this is the place to live. **It has a soul. It's a living thing**. The people who came here kept their cultures and made them a part of the fabric of New Orleans."

~ Regina Bertolino

"The similarity to where I grew up—Montreal, Canada: the weather, the **comfort zon**e of a small city without a lot of traffic. I live about two blocks from my business here in the French Quarter. Besides, I have the **opportunity to help people here.**"

~ Solomon Dawed

"New Orleans is **alive with its traditions** of all of the cultures that have lived here for years. It is both **elegant and funky** at the same time. I live in the heart of uptown where there is never a dull moment. Even sitting on the front porch can be fun."

~ Genevieve Liljeberg

A City Steeped in History

The Pontalba Apartments, built in the 1850s

"I was so grateful that the oldest parts of N.O. were not destroyed in the aftermath of Hurricane Katrina. It's so good to be able to see and touch the buildings that my father frequented. In fact, so many generations of us continue New Orleans' heritage and our **history is so evident**, when we walk down the streets I feel like everybody who was here before me is walking with us.

~ Tammy Moret

"The boundary between the living and the dead is thin in New Orleans, making it very **'spirit-u-a-l'** —not necessarily religious—somewhat like Santa Fe and Sedona. Even our graves, of necessity above ground due to soil water tables, keep us **in touch with our past and our ancestors.**"

~ Kevin Champagne

Compelling Reasons

"Not many places have the amount of **cultural activities so easy to get to** in a place that feels so **comfortable:** I can eat beignets in an outside cafe in the morning, have lunch at a very nice restaurant, and take a ride on a riverboat that afternoon. It's easy to see the French, Spanish, and many other influences. Even our public transportation—I can take a bus or enjoy the streetcar. Besides, it's such a small, compacted area; you get the feeling of a big family. I didn't get that feeling when I visited other small towns or large cities."

~ Ryan Gregoire

"It's a one-of-a-kind place compared to other places where I've traveled and lived—the history, living environment, the people, and hospitality. You get hellos when you see people; **you feel welcome here.**"   ~ Antoinette James

New Orleans has many institutions of higher education. In the 2008 *U.S. News and World Report*'s annual survey of the nation's colleges and universities, Loyola University placed first in the 'Great Schools, Great Prices' category, and Dillard, Tulane, and Xavier also received high marks. Later that year *Community College Week* named seventeen colleges in the Louisiana Community and Technical College System among the fastest-growing two-year colleges in the country.[27]

"In 1965 I got graduate fellowships to Chicago, Vanderbilt, and Tulane. I decided the climate and food would be best here. Tulane gave a good graduate education and I enjoyed the city. So when I retired, I decided to return. Despite Katrina, **I still enjoy the city,** and on bicycle I've seen new places that I didn't know existed."

~ Susan Jayne

"We attended Tulane here and just sort of stayed on afterwards for work and more graduate work at Tulane. My boyfriend jokes, 'For the food.' My initial response was, 'Because the dogs want us to live here.' In reality, **New Orleans is just somewhere that eventually goes from somewhere you go to school, and then to 'home,'** and you're not sure why — it just is."

~ Courtney Gould

"All the attractions like the paintings in the French Quarter, Blue Bayou Water Park, and our community pool."

~ Candace Navarre

"I tried out today for the New Orleans Center for Creative Arts. I've been dancing since I was one and am glad that's here."

~ Brenna Serigne

*"There are a lot of **activities you can involve your children in,** like the Children's Museum; the Hornets' games, which are really geared toward children; or Audubon Park on Sundays, where lots of people bring their dogs or play volleyball games. We also ride the streetcar down Carrolton and St. Charles, then go to the Riverwalk and have beignets and other fun."*

~ Debra Felix with son, Tevin, & daughter, Ire'

"I really like all the fun we have—all the things we can do, like coming out here to the lakefront and crabbing and fishing."

~ Chris Jackson

"You get to see historical museums. At the Cabildo I learned about the first people here—Native Americans, and I learned about the past during wars at the World War II museum. It's fun because it's an historical city."

~ Nikki Hooker

"All the activities that Kristina and I do in New Orleans—sing in the choir at church, play tennis a little, participate in Kingsley House after-school care—lots to do."

~ Kimberly Hawkins

Kristina & Kimberly Hawkins

"*I like the variety of communities in close proximity*: New Orleans has its history and the Saints football games, I think Metairie is upbeat and modern, and here in Chalmette I have a strong community full of people I know and like. I'm a senior at Chalmette High School. The 2005 hurricanes forced us to mature more quickly, which I think is a good thing. Another is that we have a chance to start over again and create something new. These are good changes for our communities."

~ Billal Jaber

"*We get New Orleans and also the country-like living in Chalmette*: We're close to a great tourist area, yet here we have a family atmosphere—we know everybody, have a cohesive group, and a strong sense of community. Unfortunately, after the hurricanes we lost a lot of our elders, but our younger population has come back."

~ Debbie Gaudet (Photo unavailable)

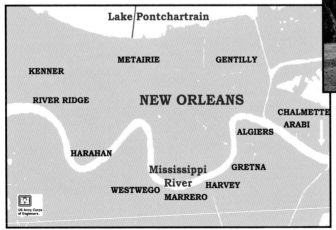

St. Bernard State Park

Chalmette
St. Bernard Parish

"We do things in New Orleans and the surrounding communities—recreation, sports, entertainment, food—*there's so much in the area*. St. Bernard Parish offers good fishing, seafood, and oil from our refineries.

Before the 2005 hurricanes we were like a big family—my family lived here, and like other families, we grew up and stayed, generation after generation. I've lived, taught, and coached here a long time, so I know a lot of people. I like the *family orientation* of our community."

~ Stephen A. Cowen III

"It's about *freedom* for me. I'm not a city person: I don't like buildings close together, traffic, and so on. However, I need a good number of businesses to be able to do my technology consulting, and I like *convenience*.

That's why I like living in Metairie. I still have all I need whenever I want it. Other smallish towns I've visited have had too many limitations on what was available or when one could access it, or it was necessary to drive long distances to get it."

~Andrès Escalante

St. Bernard Parish

It's hard to be bored with such **easy access to so much to do** in the area!

Clockwise from top center: French Market Community Flea Market, Chalmette Battlefield, Vernell Wilson fishing in West End, pedestrian walkway outside Jackson Square, volleyball court in West End, Kingsley House, Dave King in City Park

A Magical Place

"I think—and this is the truth—I think there's a magic in New Orleans. . . . There is a feeling in this city that all the people here, no matter what group they're in, they love it. They love it dearly."[28]

Ella Brennan, New Orleans Restaurateur, 2007

Our Place — and yours

"My ancestors helped settle the area. I love our New Orleans culture and our lifestyle. I really get into the music festivals we have, Mardi Gras, and our food. I've only missed two Mardi Gras days in my life. I enjoy parades the way others enjoy football games. I went to a parade in another state and the people just stood there watching it; they thought I was strange as I moved around with the music and celebration."

~ Linda Hattier

"I feel the way most people probably feel about their homes: I love it here. I was born here, traveled with the navy, and lived other places. I came back here because it's *unique* and because *I feel at home here.*"

~ William "Willie" Picket, Jr.

"It's all about *'home'*— a familiar place. We know the people here and the whole southern hospitality thing. I didn't feel that on the out-of-state trip I just had. It's personal here. You can feel the *genuineness.*"

~ Nancy Che

"My family and I have visited and lived in other places. *New Orleans gets in your soul, and the spirit of New Orleans moves you to always come back.*"

~ Mia Norflin

2004

2008

Just as New Orleans is steeped in history, our house and neighborhood in Metairie are steeped in **personal history** that gives me **a profound sense of belonging:** Having previously lived in New Orleans apartments, Dad built this house for our family in 1956. My husband and I added to my childhood history as we visited my parents over the years. After my last parent died, the uncle with whom Dad had worked in 1956 helped us update the house. A number of our neighbors are the same ones who were here then, and we still care about and look out for each other.

This personal history and sense of belonging make for hard choices. One couple born and raised in the area is considering leaving. Even though both husband and wife held professional jobs, they were unable to afford repairs to their house after Hurricane Gustav caused significant damage in 2008. That's because their insurance deductible had gone from $4,000 to $13,000 after repairs were made following hurricane Katrina's damages in 2005.

Ramona Guidry and family apparently made a different choice. In September 2008, after three hurricanes in three years hit Jean Lafitte, Louisiana, 25 miles south of New Orleans, reporter Stacey Plaisance interviewed Ramona in her childhood home where Ramona's mother still lives. Even as Ramona tried to straighten up a bit, with no water or power yet, she declared, "This is where I went to school. This is where I grew up. This is where we want to be."[29]

Our decisions to live here are not made lightly, so let's address the concerns underlying the central question prompting this book, **"Why do people live in New Orleans?"**

I can almost hear some people saying, "Yes, I understand that I and others benefit from, and even depend on, Orleanians there, and I can also appreciate its appeal, but . . .

- What about the area being below sea level, especially in a time of rising sea levels?

- What about the hurricanes, especially with the prediction of more frequent and more powerful ones?

- How long can such an area be sustained, and who pays for it?"

"Yes, but . . ." thoughts often block us from additional information, so we will pause now and address these important issues that dramatically affect us all and require a concerted effort by all to resolve.

Sea level — big picture

Local sea level has **risen** 0.4 ft (.12 m) since the 1960s, and much of New Orleans has **sunk** over 1.5 ft (.46 m) in the same period for a combined change of 2 ft (.6 m) relative to sea level.[30] Additionally, Louisiana has **lost** some 1,900 sq mi (4921 sq km) of coastal wetlands since the 1930s, accounting for up to 80% of the nation's coastal land loss, increasing vulnerability to flooding and storm surge.[31]

DEPRIVATION Extensive levee systems and upstream dams along the Mississippi River and its tributaries prevent coastal wetlands from receiving freshwater, nutrients, and sediment replenishment needed to survive and regenerate.

SUBSIDENCE, THE SINKING OF LAND

- Natural compacting of loose soil
- Earth shifts and settlement deep below ground
- Draining land for agriculture, road and canal construction, and urban development
- Weight of buildings, levees, and spoil banks
- Some believe underground strata collapse after oil and gas are extracted

SALTWATER INTRUSION

Saltwater enters canals and weakens or kills freshwater vegetation, so soil disintegrates and wetlands convert to open water.

EROSION, THE WEARING AWAY OF LAND

- Natural abrasive force of water and wind
- Logging and clear-cutting cypress swamps
- Dredging thousands of canals for navigation and oil and gas, creating miles of new shorelines for saltwater to erode
- Wind and boat wake washing away the edges and carrying off sediment

HURRICANE DAMAGE

The coastal land loss from hurricanes Katrina and Rita in 2005 amounted to roughly ten years' worth of loss in two days, with nearly half from the relatively small land area east of the lowermost Mississippi River, the buffer needed most for the protection of metropolitan New Orleans.[32]

China, India, Bangladesh, Vietnam, Indonesia, Japan, Egypt, the United States, Thailand, and the Philippines have the largest number of people living within 10 m (about 33 ft) of the average sea level.[33] Worldwide, about half of all salt marshes and mangrove swamps have been cleared, drained, diked, or filled, and few estuaries remain unpolluted or unaltered.[34] Louisiana coastal land loss is the most rapid in the United States, forming a major laboratory for global climate change;[35] what happens here and the response to it have widespread implications.

Loss of habitable land, livelihood, cultures, plant and animal species

Human factors—Imagine the heartbreak we feel as we witness the extensive loss of ecosystems, habitable land, livelihood, and cultures because of the forces described on the previous page. Ken Wells, author of *The Good Pirates of the Forgotten Bayou*, grew up on a bayou in Terrebonne Parish. He is worried about the way of life that will disappear with the bayous.[37] Many who have lived that life have a hard time envisioning another.

A 1995 publication of the Barataria-Terrebonne National Estuary Program warned that no other place on Earth was disappearing as quickly as this estuarine system.[38] Having watched it slowly surrender to the ocean, Chief Albert Naquin in 2006 recalled the Isle de Jean Charles as it had been: "trees and farmland with hard acres of green where cattle grazed, adults trapped game, and boys and girls of the Biloxi-Chitimacha tribe ran without even dampening their feet." After Hurricane Gustav hit the area in 2008, he was again trying to convince the remaining small Choctaw-related band to move, as he himself had done.[39]

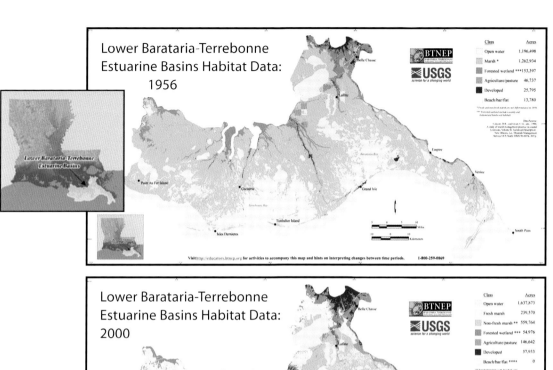

Lower Barataria-Terrebonne Estuarine Basins Habitat Data: 1956

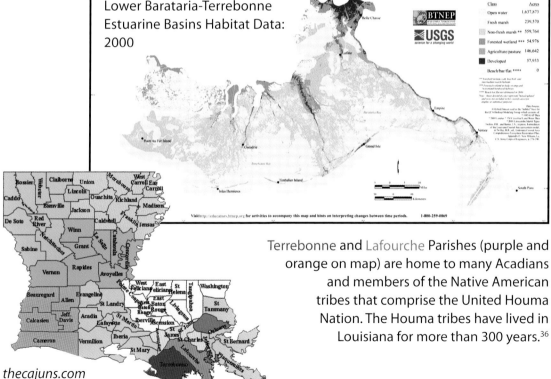

Lower Barataria-Terrebonne Estuarine Basins Habitat Data: 2000

thecajuns.com

Terrebonne and Lafourche Parishes (purple and orange on map) are home to many Acadians and members of the Native American tribes that comprise the United Houma Nation. The Houma tribes have lived in Louisiana for more than 300 years.[36]

Saltwater contamination has killed acres of freshwater cypress swamps like these in Houma, Louisiana. South Louisiana's communities remain the most vulnerable areas on the entire Gulf Coast.

Baton Rouge

Alexandria

New Orleans

Sea Level

Economic Impact—Port Fourchon, Louisiana's port on the Gulf of Mexico, services 20 percent of the nation's domestic and foreign oil supply via its docks and the Louisiana Offshore Port (LOOP). Lousiana State University economist Loren Scott "conservatively" estimates that if Port Fourchon were to shut down for just three weeks, total U.S. sales would fall by almost $10 billion, household earnings would drop by $2.9 billion, and more than 77,000 jobs would be lost.[40]

Storm protection—As the sea level rises, the protective outer delta of the Mississippi River will continue to disappear and storm surges will penetrate deeper inland with their destructive force.[41] The 2005 storm surges from Hurricanes Rita and Katrina swept across the coast at depths never considered possible and extended inland to areas once thought to be high and safe.[42] In 2008, Hurricane Gustav caused significant damage in Baton Rouge, Louisiana, (elevation 46 ft or 14 m, located about 100 mi or 160 km from the Gulf of Mexico); Alexandria, Louisiana, (elevation 75 ft or 22.9 m, located about 135 mi or 217 km from the Gulf of Mexico); and also parts of Louisiana's northern neighbor, Arkansas.[43] The same year, Hurricane Ike damaged Kentucky, northeast of Arkansas.[44] Wetlands break down waves, and delay the arrival and height of water coming in on a hurricane.

Sea Level — New Orleans area

You've already been introduced to the two bodies of water that dominate the greater New Orleans area: Lake Pontchartrain, which is slightly above sea level, and the Mississippi River, which flows about 4 ft (1.2 m) above sea level in late summer, and about 12–14 ft (3.7–4.3 m) during spring thaw.[45] **There is an incorrect impression that everything in between is below sea level and that these levels determine flooding.**

> "... 51% of the terrestrial surface of the contiguous urbanized portions of New Orleans, Jefferson, and St. Bernard parishes lie at or above mean sea level, with the highest neighborhoods at ten to twelve feet (3.05–3.66 m) above ..."[46]

Tulane and Xavier Universities' Center for Bioenvironmental Research, 2007

Reporting these facts, journalist Leslie Williams observed: Elevation did not determine flooding after Hurricane Katrina—the location and severity of levee failures and failed pumps flooded some parts that were above sea level and left some dry that were below sea level.[47]

However, the bowl-like results of the levees and bodies of water being higher than land levels prevented floodwaters from draining. Therefore, flooding lasted more than a month in some areas of New Orleans because of the need to await the repair of both the levees and pump systems before the water that collected during the storm could be removed.[48]

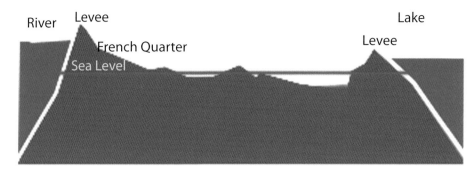

Approximation only; not precise representation

From Jackson Square in the French Quarter, one must walk up these steps to get over the inner levee protecting the city from the Mississippi River. Standing at street level, one looks up to see ships passing on the river.

More frequent and powerful hurricanes

Trend data confirms what most daily newspapers and many people's experiences have revealed: natural disasters have increased globally.[49] That's been abundantly clear in Louisiana and the New Orleans area.

"It's safe to say everyone here — okay, almost everyone—gets it now. The precariousness of life, leisure, and liberty has been driven home."[50]

~ Chris Rose, 2008

Since the French Colonial Period a hurricane has affected Louisiana at an average rate of once every three years.[51] Fortunately, the most damaging hurricanes came much less frequently. That's why my family, like a lot of others, didn't evacuate for many. Now we leave for any headed this way, given enough warning.

Many of us cling to a belief that, unlike earthquakes and other disasters, at least we know a hurricane's coming, so we can get out of harm's way, even though hurricanes have always had the propensity to change course at the last minute. Unfortunately, advance-notice time has narrowed in recent instances of hurricanes building rapidly, and defining *harm's way* is more difficult given hurricanes' emerging ability to impact areas well outside the projected path, as we experienced with Ike, the last 2008 hurricane in our area.

This need for increased mobility is troublesome for many reasons. As was highly publicized after Katrina, mobility is difficult and sometimes untenable for elders, the infirm, and people in poverty; in fact, the increased frequency and cumulative effects are also significantly challenging middle-income residents. In addition, evacuation is currently dependent on gasoline—a problematic and disappearing energy source. These and other practical and emotional decisions that accompany such a mobile lifestyle are some of residents' considerations when choosing whether to continue to live in the area.

Sustainability and regeneration of the land

Sustainability: maintenance by reduction in damage caused by excessive resource use. **Regeneration**: participating with the environment in an integrated way so it can regenerate its health and our own.[52]

Given the challenges of sea level, subsidence, erosion, hurricanes, and so on, is the New Orleans area a defensible area in which to live? The articles I've read and scientists and specialists with whom I've spoken give a cautious response of maybe, if we responsibly, intelligently, and consistently apply concerted actions at the local, state, national, and global levels, and if we don't get a direct hit from a monster hurricane while trying to make that happen.

> . . . a pervasive risk . . . more and more people and property at risk . . . an order of magnitude greater than during the previous three decades.
>
> . . . global warming and associated climate change have the potential to increase the severity and extent of . . . will lead to increases in the frequency of . . . and . . . a lengthened . . . season.[53]
>
> Lawrence Berkeley, National Laboratory's Environmental Energy Technologies Division Newsletter, Winter-Spring 2001–2002

The descriptors above seem to say that a risky place to live is getting riskier, right? They do, but they're describing wildfires in California. A lot of people live in risky places. In fact, because a lot more people now live in risky places that are getting riskier, it becomes less and less possible to choose total abandonment over informed, coordinated action.

Are there feasible actions that can prolong the New Orleans area's habitability? Yes, if we work together towards regeneration. Improving levee protection for the greater New Orleans area without coastal restoration is futile, as is depending on expenditures for uncoordinated projects, or thinking Louisiana can do this without concerted efforts by the national and international communities. The events that are occurring here and elsewhere are demanding we heed our basic understanding of the term *interdependence*..

Available from the Lake Pontchartrain Basin Foundation at http://www.saveourlake.org/

COASTAL RESTORATION + LEVEES = HURRICANE PROTECTION

"Without the coast, there is no way to sustain the New Orleans metropolitan region."[54]

Carlton Dufrechou, The Lake Pontchartrain Basin Foundation, 2008

Who Pays? *We all do, of course!*

"If we cannot see how what we are doing or not doing is contributing to things being the way that they are, to the system producing the results it is now producing, then it follows that we have no basis at all for changing these results— except from the outside, violently."[55]
~ Adam Kahane, "The Language of Power and the Language of Love, Solving Tough Problems in Practice," 2007

In September 2008, an American blogger named David wrote: "If you choose to live in a floodplain and within a system of levees you believe are suspect, don't expect my tax dollars to further subsidize the consequences of your decision."[56] His thinking is echoed in the national debates of the U.S. Congress each time they consider after-the-fact funding for an area of the nation that has been hit by a natural disaster. These are understandable responses if one ignores two facts:

- the interdependence governing our life on this planet, and
- the superior effectiveness of systemic planning, problem-solving, and funding over fragmented, partially-funded actions, which also cost more long term.

Interdependence

- Is the rest of the nation prepared for the social, political, environmental, and economic impact of the numbers of people who would need to relocate if southeastern Louisiana becomes uninhabitable?
- When hurricanes penetrate further inland once southern Louisiana is no longer the buffer, will the nation still debate the worthiness of systemic planning, problem solving, and funding?
- Are U.S. and global citizens willing to do without the resources described on previous pages—and to pay to relocate existing infrastructures that support, supply, or transport those resources?
- What will it take for humans to realize that the way we live affects everyone and everything on the planet? There would be no need for drilling and dredging in Louisiana, or for the massive amounts of energy used to refine oil, if people across the United States didn't depend on it. There would be no need for navigational canals if U.S. and world trade didn't depend on them. There would be no need for the wetlands if species from around the world didn't depend on them and we didn't depend on those species, or if we didn't depend on the many other functions the wetlands perform.

> *"One way or the other, the earth is going to teach us that we are an organic part of the whole. The earth is going to reveal to us just how profound our connections are to the whole of humanity and to the profoundly broken and abused webs of life. We can choose to cooperate with those systems in order to salvage human life, or the earth will be forced to adjust to the new reality we have presented it, finding a new equilibrium among these broken systems. Scientists tell us this new equilibrium may or may not allow for the survival of the human species."*[57]
> ~ Margaret Swedish, *Living Beyond the "End of the World,"* 2008

Sound like an extreme statement—even with these concrete consequences of our actions: the disappearance of the Louisiana coast and its inhabitants after damming the river that was its source of replenishment, and cutting up and siphoning the remaining land for commerce and agriculture? Let's examine another example.

"What happens to the coasts has effects that reach far beyond their local aquatic and human communities."[58]

~ Peter Weber, *"It Comes Down to the Coasts,"* 2008

Interdependence (continued)

Water pollution also demonstrates our individual responsibility and mutual dependence. In 2007, researchers identified over 200 "dead zones" around the world's coastlines, an increase of 51 such zones since 2003.[59] "Dead zones" are areas where the dissolved oxygen levels are so low that no marine life other than microorganisms can be sustained.

The world's largest is in the Baltic Sea, covering some 70,000 square kilometers of seabed. The second-largest dead zone is in the Gulf of Mexico. It covers 21,000 square kilometers, an area the size of New Jersey.[60] Much of the nitrogen that fuels the hypoxia (oxygen depletion) comes from north of the confluence of the Mississippi and Ohio Rivers.[61]

Don Hinrichsen notes that ocean currents act as Earth's super highways, transferring enormous quantities of water and nutrients from one place to another. The Gulf Stream, for instance, pushes more water from the Gulf of Mexico and the Caribbean across the Atlantic into northern Europe than is carried by all the rivers on earth. Ocean currents also transport pollutants into the remotest corners of the world's seas.[62]

This may be another reason why visitors frequently include international scientists, policymakers, and media professionals who want to see the condition of Louisiana's coast firsthand.[63] Our challenges, and similar ones around the world, were not caused exclusively by locals, are not experienced exclusively by locals, and cannot be resolved exclusively by locals.

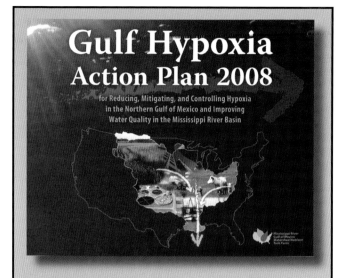

Interdependence. This cover of the Gulf Hypoxia Action Plan 2008, prepared by the Mississippi River/Gulf of Mexico Watershed Task Force, helps us visualize our mutual stake in events occurring in this area.

1)   Nitrogen and phosphorous enter the river through upstream runoff of fertilizers, soil erosion, animal wastes, and sewage.
2)   Fewer wetlands are available to filter these pollutants, which are dumped into the Gulf of Mexico, where they form "dead zones," create massive fish kills, and alter the food chain.
3)   Currents transport the pollutants into the ocean and across the globe.

Who Pays? *We all do, of course!*

"Coastal and ocean areas can be managed sustainably . . . only if concerted efforts can be made by national governments and the international community, acting together and working together toward a common set of objectives." [64]

~ Don Hinrichsen, "Ocean Planet in Decline," 2008

Systemic Effectiveness

After 1927 flooding, the nation completely funded a system of protection of the Lower Mississippi Valley and its maintenance thereafter. Although the chosen design of the protection is now in question, the systemic planning, funding, and follow-through continue to serve their goals sixty years later.

Coastal protection systems, however, have never been fully funded and were not funded as an integrated system. They have proceeded in fits and starts and have been subject to other local or federal economic development priorities.[65] Moreover, we have seen that coastal protection must lead to coastal regeneration.

Mark Davis, senior research fellow and director of the Tulane Institute on Water Resources Law and Policy at Tulane Law School states, "... restoring our coast and by extension protecting the social, economic and ecological life of the region . . . will require leadership from the top—mayors, our governor, agency heads and even the president—and it will require persistent pressure from the public."[66] Our knowledge of interdependence tells us that the international community has a stake in exerting such leadership and pressure, too.

Almost half the Netherlands lies below sea level, and its lowest point is much lower than New Orleans' 9th Ward. About twice the size of New Jersey, it is one of the most densely populated countries in the world.[67]

Prime Minister Balkenende explained at a speech in Spain in 2008, "Keeping people's feet dry has always been one of the main tasks of the Dutch government."[68]

Dale Morris, an economic adviser with the Dutch embassy in Washington, was in New Orleans later that year. He added that this national approach to living with water attracts business and encourages prosperity. Investors see the Netherlands as a good bet.[69]

There is no debate in the Netherlands on the need for action as a nation.[70]

Our means of payment are consistent, informed, individual actions and persistent pressure for organized, systemic effectiveness worldwide, and we must accelerate both to match the urgency evident in this region.

Informed Action in Louisiana

"It is up to us as individuals and local governments, to take the lead in protecting our lives and property and to establish resilient and sustainable communities."[71]

~ J. G. Wilkins, R. E. Emmer, D. J. Hwang, G. P. Kemp, B. Kennedy, M. Hassan, and B. Sharky, *Louisiana Coastal Hazard Mitigation Guidebook*, 2008

"Southeastern Louisiana must make excruciating choices regarding people, culture, and place if it is to survive. Entangled in those decisions are problems involving coastal restoration, economic diversification, environmental sustainability, social equity, and learning to live with risk. As a geographer, I believe these problems are solvable, so long as citizens muster the will to tackle them and the courage to confront the dilemmas underlying them."[72]

~ Richard Campanella, *Bienville's Dilemma*, 2008

Like citizens across the globe, we need courage to weigh individual interests and practices against those that regenerate the place we want to inhabit, short-term needs against long-term solutions, norms of doing things to nature versus participating with it, and habits of making changes that allow the dysfunctional system to continue versus changing the system itself. The choices cross economic and social boundaries of all kinds, so we need to ensure that wise choices are also economically and otherwise feasible for all.

Louisiana Coastal Hazard Mitigation Guidebook

Suggested Use of the Guidebook

- Citizens & developers: to become better informed of the natural hazards they face and what they can do to protect themselves and their customers
- Local governments: to become better planners and protectors of the communities they govern

Available at: http://www.lsu.edu/sglegal

MULTIPLE LINES OF DEFENSE (coastal restoration & man-made defenses like raised houses and levees) + ZONING AND LAND-USE PLANNING = HAZARD MITIGATION

A number of New Orleans homes look huge because they have been raised since 2005 Hurricanes Katrina and Rita. The bottom floors are often non-livable and uninsurable spaces.

Why do people live in the New Orleans area?

Can you answer the question yet? Now you have a number of facts at your fingertips to explain the practical reasons, and you have some insight into why residents find the place so appealing. However, given the concerns we've just raised, you might be better prepared with a more complete view of residents' reasons.

From "yes, but . . ." to "yes, and . . ."

Yes, we're fully aware of the area's challenges, and in the next pages residents will share some very strong reasons that keep us here, working to regenerate the area.

The People

Ella Brennan mentioned how the groups—our diverse people with unique cultures—are united by their love of the overall New Orleans culture. Conflict is a natural ingredient of any group or mixture of groups, so sometimes individuals in those groups conflict. Yet, these next pages will show that it is the simultaneous friendliness of people across groups, celebration of diversity, acceptance of individuality, and desire for community that in large part define New Orleans' culture. These ever-present, seemingly dichotomous forces and the resultant passion for New Orleans are assets we must call upon and strengthen to regenerate the area and the planet.

The People — friendliness

If I answer the phone and someone addresses me as "Mrs. Ewy," it's probable that the person is not local. Locals, such as a grocery store cashier reading my name from my I.D., would say "Miss Christine." It's warm and respectful, similar to the rejoinders often heard: "Yes, Ma'am," and "Yes, Sir." If someone walks by, they're not only apt to greet you, but as these residents explain, they're apt to stop and have a conversation.

Compelling Reasons

"I was born here. I like to travel and see other places, but I can't wait to get back. I like the people and the culture. *People are friendly.* I can be at a shopping center and hold a conversation with almost anyone."

~ Marilyn O'Connor

"There's a lot to do here and a lot of people in the community. There's a welcoming kind of feeling; everybody's friendly. A lot of people don't care if you're white, black, or another color or race; *you're kind of like family.* Why would you want to leave if you have fun?"

~ Zachary Danna

"My mom's from here, and when I was 14, my father retired from the military and we came here. People here are so much more friendly; *you don't have to know someone to talk to them or strike up a conversation.* Other places I've been the people are not as open as here."

~ Inez Ball

"I love living in New Orleans because many clichés you hear about New Orleans are true—*people are warm and friendly, and a lot of other little things.* Even Mardi Gras makes a difference because many people in the area are having a similar experience at the same time, bringing us together."

~ Sharon Shih (photo unavailable)

"*King Tut! The New Orleans Museum of Art exhibit was a huge success with hours spent in line. Problem? No, not to the people of New Orleans. A spontaneous block party broke out in line with coolers of shared sandwiches and cold beer. 'Watcha need, darlin'?' Love, New Orleans-style, is all about food, family, and* events made special by total strangers."

~ Donald K. Midkiff

"*My parents' divorce placed me in New Orleans when I was ten years old. Though I visited New England each summer, I considered New Orleans my home.* I feel comfort and love here, *enjoy the history, the links to South and Central America and the Caribbean. The diversity is stimulating, as are the music, food, and neighborhoods.*"

~ Helena Midkiff

Ellen & Jesse Hardeman attending the Japan Festival at the New Orleans Museum of Art

Diversity - our heritage

People often associate the French language with our city. After all, the French settled and later sold *La Nouvelle Orléans*; the French Quarter, or *Vieux Carré*, is its historical center; and there is our Acadian, or Cajun, French-speaking heritage. However, the first pages of this book confirmed the early Native American and later Spanish influences. In fact, even these are only part of the rich blend of people, languages, and cultures we enjoy.

My father's ancestors, Sydney and Harriet Polk, were Native Americans from the Choctaw tribe

The People — diversity

Here are a few facts about early cultural influences on our state, taken from *The Encyclopedia of Cajun & Creole Cuisine* by John Folse.[73]

- France brought slaves from West Africa who provided labor and knowledge of rice cultivation.

- Spain recruited Canary Islanders to help protect and settle Louisiana.

- Haitian refugees brought new sugarcane varieties.

- New Orleans was the second leading port of entry for Germans fleeing wars in their home country. (The German surname "Foltz" was changed in Louisiana to "Folse.")

- Rosedown Plantation is an example of English influence in Louisiana.

- After the Civil War, Italians from southern mainland Italy and Sicily were recruited to work on plantations. In 1880, about 7% of the retail grocers in New Orleans were Italians. By 1913, Italians dominated the businesses through which 73 million tons of produce were exported to Latin America.

"I love our culture. We have many types of people, so we get to experience so much more than other places. Because of this the food and festivals are different, some that others never heard of, and they come here to experience what we live every day."

~ Inez Ball (Photo on page 48)

My maternal grandfather, Rosario Salvaggio, behind the counter in his grocery store in New Orleans

Valued aspects of New Orleans culture - Besides the people and languages that bear witness to our continued diversity, one need only observe our street signs, architecture, delicious food, and great music!

Okra
(oh-krə)
"gombo"

Filé
(fee-lay)
"kombo"

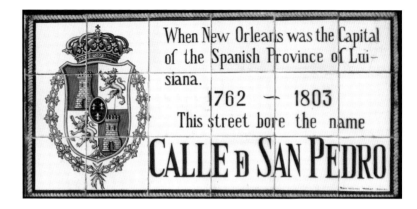

The bowl of gumbo above, for example, apparently has **French, African,** and **Native American** origins. It has some qualities of the **French soup, bouillabaisse,** and it uses **okra—called "gombo" by Africans, filé—called "kombo" by the Choctaw Indians,** and whatever else the cooks can easily get to put into it.[74] My personal favorite is seafood gumbo.

Our music, too, evolved from multiple cultures. Jazz and Jazz Funerals developed from a mixture of **African** and European traditions. (Jazz Funerals are the unique musical processions following a casket to burial.)[75] African-American artists such as Jelly Roll Morton, Duke Ellington, Louis Armstrong, and Count Basie had a large influence on jazz. Throughout time many ethnic groups in New Orleans contributed.

Later, local artists such as Fats Domino, Irma Thomas, and Dr. John added a New Orleans flavor to rhythm and blues, which combines jazz, gospel, and blues. Zydeco music, imported from our southwest Louisiana neighbors, highlights our **Canadian French Acadian,** or **Cajun,** culture.

The People — diversity

Compelling Reasons

"After the 2005 hurricane, I had offers to open my restaurant in Atlanta and southern Florida, but there was no question that I wanted to stay here in the French Quarter. I love the food, people, and culture, as well as the love of restaurants that I have in common with people here."

~ James Ritchie, Owner, Louisiana Pizza Kitchen

Louisiana Pizza Kitchen was not flooded, but personnel didn't fare as well. For six months James Ritchie housed Yukita Porter and two other workers who had lost everything in the hurricane's aftermath. The restaurant, therefore, was the second one in the French Quarter to reopen.

Another restaurateur apparently has similar feelings as James Ritchie. Middendorf's is located about forty miles from New Orleans, west of Lake Pontchartrain on Lake Maurepas. In September of 2008, at least four feet of water surge from Hurricane Ike badly damaged this Manchac seafood restaurant known for its catfish. According to Liz Reyes, an ABC26 anchor-reporter, owner Horst Pfeiffer said he decided to rebuild because he was too committed to the business, his employees, and the community to walk away from it. This decision was even more significant because a previous New Orleans restaurant that he owned, the Bella Luna, had been closed after damage from Hurricane Katrina and subsequent looting.[76]

Compelling Reasons

"I enjoy the music, and while I'm listening to it, I can eat good food."

~ Ernest Rogers

"The number of places that have good food here—'hole-in-the-wall' places as well as others—spoils me rotten. When I travel I miss that good food."

~ Linda Hattier (Photo on page 32)

Great Music!

This is another example of the easy access we have in New Orleans to things that make us happy. We can find music almost anywhere, every day, for every occasion, representing our wide variety of cultures. For example, we can sample zydeco, jazz, blues, and more in one of the many land venues with live music, sway to the rhythms of the Dukes of Dixieland on the steamboat *Natchez*, or listen to the Louisiana Philharmonic Orchestra in City Park.

Clockwise from left: Zydeco Band, Bassist Everett Link, the steamboat *Natchez*, Philharmonic Orchestra in City Park

The People — diversity

We can also be serenaded walking along the river, clap our hands to street musicians, or attend one of the festivals held throughout the year, many free to the public. In fact, this is one of the few places where you'll find a live band playing at an outdoor local expo for storm protection, or leading a dancing line of people to the music of a Jazz Funeral. Music and food go together at most any gathering in this city, and passersby are usually invited to enthusiastically join in.

" . . . There's no separation between music and people; when music is just happening and people can walk by and it can affect them, . . . this is an opportunity for us to really find a way to bring people together. . . . Music opens up these doors that ordinarily wouldn't be opened." [77]

~ Mark Johnson, *Playing for Change: Peace through Music*, 2008

The People — community

Orleanians find lots of reasons to celebrate, and each celebration is an opportunity to build community. Neighbors, friends, and families renew ties and meet new people as they spend hours together at parades, festivals, and events such as these.

While celebrating Tet Nguyen Dan, Thanh Vu explained why he lives here:

"My parents brought me here from Indiana. They liked the weather, similar to Viet Nam. I stay here because my family is here."

~ Thanh Vu

Family Fun At Mardi Gras Will (left), Daniel, and Geena Escalante; Bambi Fields; and Sophia De Wald (top)

"We came here in 2006 for work reasons. Discovering that our U.S. assignment was to be New Orleans conjured images of rich history, unique musical heritage, and world-renowned cuisine, as well as an uncertainty over what post-Katrina 'N'Awlins' would be like. We found one of the warmest welcomes ever in our world travels, a sense of family, community, faith, and a belief in the cause to rebuild, which has been inspirational . . . oh, and the best St. Paddy's Day this Irishman has ever seen!"

~ Paul and Kate Pickering

Some people think the **Irish-Italian Parade** each year in March is more fun than Mardi Gras day. People on decorated trucks throw cabbages, potatoes, pasta, and other food items, in addition to beads such as these.

One of the St. Joseph altars my parents had in our home

Diversity & Community

Many Orleanians of Italian heritage continue the Sicilian custom of building an altar in honor of St. Joseph on March 19. This is another of New Orleans' **many community-building events,** for it takes the help of many friends and relatives to cook all the food that goes on the altar, and later the entire community is invited to eat or take food home from it. For 100 years Angelo Brocato's has made wonderful Italian ice cream, cannoli, and cookies—many for St. Joseph Altars. It is such a popular gathering spot that, after being flooded in 2005, customers convinced the owners to rebuild, and their loyalty continues today. Frequently I join two separate groups who meet weekly to informally develop and retain their Italian language. Though some people are regulars and others drop in, these groups add to my feeling of belonging to a community.

Above: Angelo Brocato's Italian Ice Cream Parlor
Below: Part of one of the Italian language groups that meet weekly to continue their Italian language and interests

Our People

Generations of my father's family have lived here, beginning with his Native American great-grandparents. My mother was one of 10 children of immigrant parents. Our family reunion this year brought 65 of us together. After growing up surrounded by all this family, I found it extremely lonely living elsewhere for some of my adult years. We know that we have a treasured network of family and friends around the world, but the allure of New Orleans for us is the concentration of family and lifelong friends in one area, similar to others who have expressed their views in this book. Many Orleanians hold dear our value of **strong ties with family and friends.**

Family Reunion

"After the 2005 hurricanes we came back for my mom's job; she was Clerk of Council for St. Bernard Parish. Our house was still intact and, because of the strong community here, we felt we could come back and rebuild. I was so glad because I grew up here, so I have family members, friends, teachers I've known, and the community I've known. Strong friendships and shared experiences help us help each other."

~ Sophie Boudreaux

Compelling Reasons

"I was born and raised here, but left when I was older and married. I returned to have help with my children from **my mother**. Now **my daughter** loves it here, and I need to be here to help my mother."

~ Beverly Carter

"I came because I had **relatives** here. The longer I lived here, the more I liked the **laid-back and comfortable feeling**. Now I've been here 22 years."

~ Lee Yu

"Everyone is **connected** in Kenilworth because their families have been in this area for generations. You either know someone personally or you know someone who knows him. Some of our neighbors actually grew up in outlying areas, like Ycloskey, and had to move in after the hurricanes, but my son and I know everyone on our street. **We feel comfortable and safe.**

When we moved away after the storms, my eleven-year-old son had problems in school and developed an ulcer. When we returned, even though we were in a trailer at first, he immediately began to get better and is doing fine now. A neighborhood and **community made up of family and long-time friends is that important to us.**"

~ Sharon Cooper

Lifestyle

Diversity is also evident in each neighborhood. These Garden District homes are within a couple blocks of each other, and are only a few of the house styles and lifestyles there. Such **endless variety** always fascinates me on my walks.

Acceptance of individuality

The **coexistence** of these examples from our own neighborhood is in keeping with the **"little town" informality** I described earlier. It may be part of how people from the New Orleans area earned the term *laid-back.*

In addition to the mixture of house types in close proximity, the streets themselves vary. Below, one house sits on an asphalt street, and the other on a cement-paved street with curbs. They are a block apart.

Lifestyle

Perhaps we don't want everything to look alike because we **savor** a certain amount of **imperfection** while simultaneously striving to improve our area. For me the imperfection is integral to the authenticity of the New Orleans experience.

We work for strong levees and coastal restoration because the beauty of nature is so accessible on our unmanicured shores.

We build new venues for jazz and other performances, and we keep Preservation Hall.

We build a modern, impressive bank and retain the snowball stand right next to it.

"Born and raised here, I've lived in three other sates. Other places I've been don't have the same feel, the same food, or the same spirit. You feel free here. In some other places, for example, you couldn't even bring your dog to the park, but here we are enjoying the lakefront with food, an ice chest, music, and a dog if we wanted."

~ Norman Jackson

"There is a warmth here, a feel to it that you don't get anywhere else. The people are alive with personality. Our diversity enriches us. We find many ways to celebrate what we have despite everything. We even celebrate the afterlife with our second-line parades at Jazz Funerals."

~ Lily and Tammy Moret

The people interviewed in this book come from across the greater New Orleans area, representing different geographic, ethnic, socioeconomic, gender, and age groups. I sought diverse viewpoints. Yet, differences did not show up when I recorded their words; commonalities did.

For us, **there's no other place quite like the New Orleans area,** so we join the efforts of our coastal neighbors and people around the globe to improve our world in order to enjoy it for many years to come. This local persistence and global joint-effort yield even greater compelling reasons for people to live here.

Call To Action

"I think it has genuinely come as a surprise for people to discover that we have collectively managed to do damage to the entire planet. We never dreamed that we'd have power to influence anything so big."[78]

~ Gerald Barney, Our Task, Inc., 2007

On page 28 Billal Jaber said he thought the 2005 hurricanes forced Chalmette High School students to mature more quickly, which he thought was a good thing. In a sense, the challenges we face around the world are forcing all of us to mature and stop living such contradictions as these local examples illustrate.

- If we say we want our drainage system to protect us from flooding, then we can't throw leaves, Mardi Gras throws, or trash into the drains, streets, canals, or basins.

- If we want our land to be for food, residences, recreation, and business instead of landfills, then we must recycle and reuse, rather than buying more and more and discarding it.

- If we love our seafood, local game, and the livelihood they bring, then we need to heed limit restrictions and encourage others to do the same, rather than killing for sport or depleting our supplies.

- If we say we love the natural beauty of our area, then we can no longer leave our litter and trash behind us. In fact, we might keep a bag with us to clean up places we frequent.

- If we recognize Lake Pontchartrain's increasing effects on us during hurricanes due to adjacent land loss and subsidence, and we also love the lake's beauty and recreational value, we can't lift the moratorium on placing more oil wells there.

- If we know that Louisiana leads the country in feeling the effects of global warming, we must become leaders in curbing dependence on oil and lowering greenhouse gases.

"I like our pretty land. If we had garbage and litter every-where, we wouldn't have enough places to live and play. We wouldn't have a clean community."

~ Michael Villafranco

Those who have asked why people live here either didn't know or had forgotten the national and global dependence upon this area, and therefore, the need for stewards here. In turn, those of us who live here, like our global counterparts, have repeatedly forgotten our dependence on our environment for our very existence. We have for a long time been saying, "We'll take care of our environment when we're in a better financial position," but we know from our disappearing land and frantic efforts for hurricane protection that the future is here. As difficult as financial considerations make our choices, we have arrived, especially in southern Louisiana, at a time when **every choice we make must ensure a healthy environment** if we want to continue to live in and benefit from this area. We must . . .

1. **Make personal, daily choices that cooperate with and heal our environment.** Examples: stop the contradictions listed on the previous page, use facts from this book or other sources to stop the debate on whether New Orleans and its global counterparts need everyone's efforts, and follow the long-standing advice to "Think globally and act locally."

2. **Become informed, active citizens to ensure your influence on local, regional, national, and world leaders and developments.** Vote only for people who will regenerate our area and planet, write letters to the editor on related issues, and sign online petitions for the environment are some ways.

3. **Join with others to take action in whatever way your time, finances, and life circumstances permit,** whether it be with your extended family, neighbors, neighborhood civic association, groups listed in this book's Related Resources, or other possibilities.

Many current residents of the New Orleans area are uniquely qualified stewards of our homeland: we have generations-deep knowledge of its geography and history, heightened motivation from a love of place strengthened by threats of losing it, and renewed determination as evidenced by our repeated choice to remain here and our increased activism. **We, the nation, and the world need only join those described on the next pages to do what it takes to regenerate this exquisite area.**

"Community is the unit of change. The only way we get through difficult times is together."[79]

~ Margaret Wheatley, 2008

Residents throughout this book have shown that community is their source of joy in good times and strength in tough times Journalist Chris Rose noted that ". . . in the wake of Hurricane Katrina, . . . a large-scale sense of activism and ownership took hold of the masses."[80]

A few examples . . .

The City Park "Mow-Rons" voluntarily cut the park's grass; Carey Shea was dubbed "the bench fairy" because she took it upon herself to make and place benches for people to sit on at bus stops; and for two years after Katrina, Emily Posner, a farmer from Maine, used sunflowers and other means to remove toxins from the city's soil to create long-term health and sustainability. Malik Rahim, co-founder of Common Ground Collective, a relief organization made up of locals and volunteers from around the world, shares some results of other examples: *"We have challenged and have broken the stereotype of racial divide. We have had over 10,000 volunteers, with maybe over 9,000 being Caucasians working in African-American and minority communities. . . . We can make this a better world. It's all about restoring hope."*[81]

"... A lot of people are living in a world of fear, but we don't even know how long we're going to be in this world, so there's really no reason to fear anything. The most important thing is while we're here, let's make a difference together."[82]

~ Mark Johnson, Playing for Change: Peace Through Music, 2008

People who want to make a difference together know they can do so in the New Orleans area. They know they can contribute to humanity and the environment in concrete ways with whatever time or resources they want to offer. The area has become a vehicle for civic-minded people to be proactive, so they don't waste time debating the area's sustainability; they show up to help regenerate it. We have been blessed with many **volunteers** to help since the 2005 hurricanes. In fact, it was estimated at over a million people by August 2007 and they are still coming. Here are two examples of why **we are deeply grateful to each of them.**

Some Mormon men from Texas arrived on our street in early October 2005 with a truck and equipment, asking if they could help us with storm debris. They removed a large limb from our roof, cut up a toppled tree in my neighbor's yard, and continued around the neighborhood. They wouldn't take so much as a bottle of water for their labor.

A FEMA worker learned that my cousin had more pressing financial needs than fixing her flooded home because shortly after the flood she discovered she had cancer. This worker promptly stunned my cousin by writing out a check from his personal account to the hospital, making it possible for her to continue her chemotherapy.

"The only choice we have is to come together and to inspire each other, because that's the way that we'll create a better world for us now and for the kids tomorrow."[83]

~ Mark Johnson, Playing for Change: Peace Through Music, 2008

Here are just a few more examples of why we are grateful to people from all over the United States and the world. Please show this to anyone you know who has helped, and explain that, though I only speak these four languages, I hope my heart's thank you is clear. All of these people inspire us.

Locals, informally and in organized groups, help each other rebuild houses and lives.
Friends, relatives, and strangers offer refuge and assistance.
Canadian first-responders arrive days after disaster; others follow.
Volunteers rescue animals and try to reconnect them with owners.
Leaders and their countrymen from around the world offer broad and specific help.
Distant fishermen, firefighters, educators, and others help their N.O. counterparts.
Countless convention-goers add days to their visit to help locals rebuild.
Children individually, in schools, & in other groups actively contribute.
Students come on their holiday break, and
Couples come on their honeymoon to help
And so much more!

Grazie Mille!
Merci Beaucoup!
Thank You Very Much!
¡Muchisimas Gracias!

High school and professional musicians
College and professional athletes
Brad Pitt, Ellen Degeneres, and other celebrities
West Point cadets and officers
Red Cross, United Way, Volunteers of America
Bill Gates, Leonard Riggio, and other philanthropists
Families of 9/11 and Oklahoma bombings
Rabbis, pastors, congregations
Former U.S. Presidents
Habitat for Humanity
And so many more!

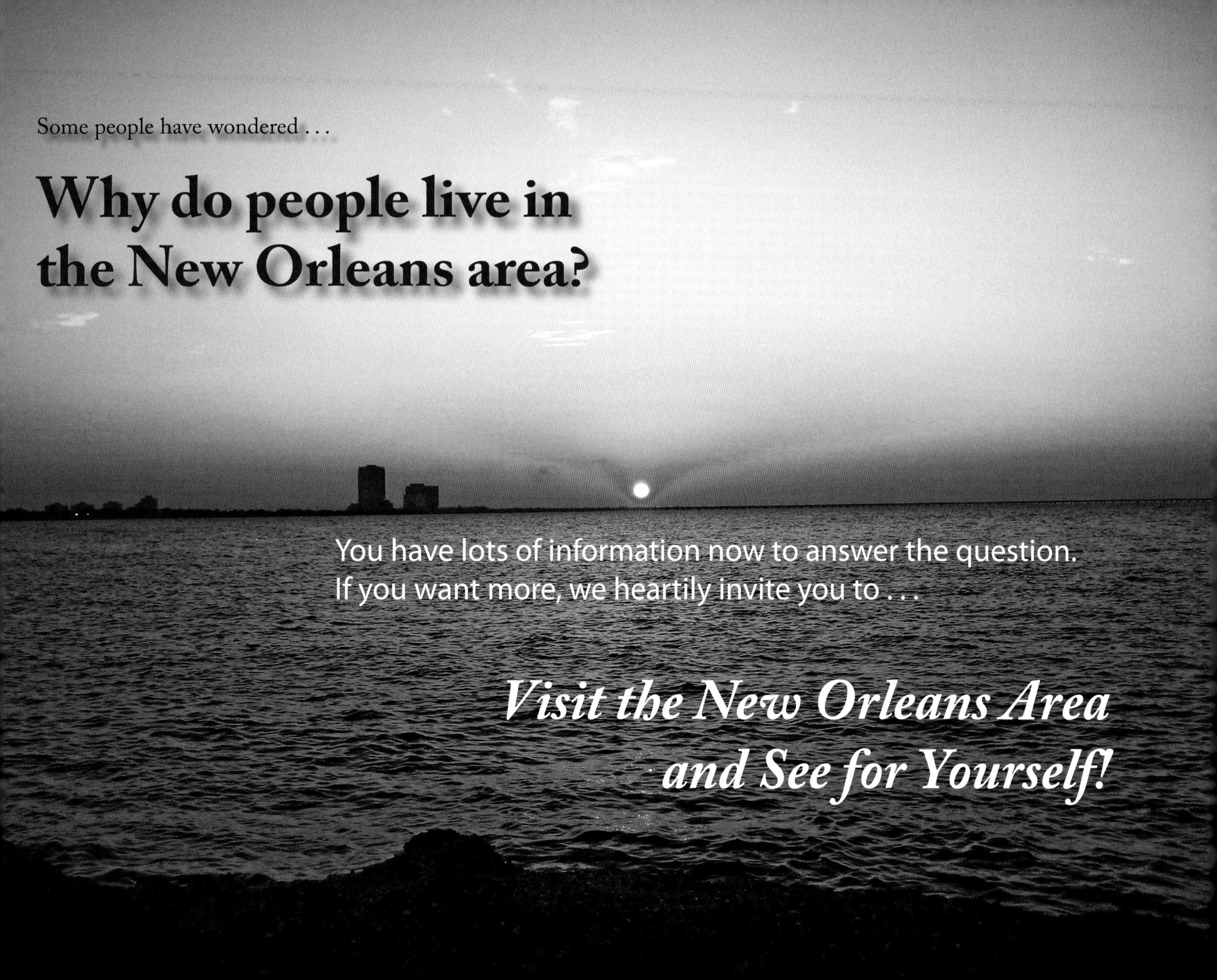
Some people have wondered . . .
Why do people live in the New Orleans area?
You have lots of information now to answer the question.
If you want more, we heartily invite you to . . .
Visit the New Orleans Area and See for Yourself!

Your Pages

After this page you'll find the Notes, Related Resources, and Index, but I don't want you to miss pages 83–86. They continue our custom of giving lagniappe—a little something extra with your purchase. In this case, it's a place to add (or enlarge if you are already quoted) a vital voice to this book: your own.

You are welcome to place on these pages your own photos, reasons you live in New Orleans or wherever you live, or memories of experiences from when you were in the New Orleans area. Then you'll have more resources in one place to discuss why people live here and how that matters to you and others.

Another Possibility

A portion of the proceeds from the sale of these books will be used to give books to volunteers as a thank-you for the work they have done in the New Orleans area. Unfortunately, I cannot possibly know, much less send books to, all volunteers. Perhaps, then, after you've read your book, you might give it or another to a volunteer whom you know has helped here or elsewhere. If so, these pages would be perfect for you, your family, and others to write a personal thank-you note inside a gift from you that reflects the volunteer's connection with you. If you choose this option, I thank you in advance for expanding this chorus of gratitude from New Orleans.

Notes

1   Peter Weber, *It Comes Down to the Coasts*, World Watch, vol. 7 No.2, reprinted in San Diego Earth Times Aug '94, http://www.sdearthtimes.com/et0894/et0894s5.html (March 13, 2009); National Ocean and Atmospheric Administration, U.S. Department of Commerce, *Coasts*, http://www.noaa. gov/coasts.html, (March 18, 2009).

2   Peter Weber, http://www.sdearthtimes.com/et0894/et0894s5.html.

3   Don Hinrichsen, *Ocean Planet in Decline* (overview article) in People and Planet, February 19, 2008, http://www.peopleandplanet.net/doc.php?id=429&section=6 (November 26, 2008).

4   U.S Environmental Protection Agency, Gulf of Mexico Program, *General Facts about the Gulf of Mexico*, http://epa.gov/gmpo/about/facts.html Last updated on Friday, June 6, 2008. (September 24, 2008).

5   Peter Weber, *It Comes Down to the Coasts*, http://www.sdearthtimes.com/et0894/350894s5.html.

6   Peirce F. Lewis, *New Orleans, The Making of an Urban Landscape* (Santa Fe, New Mexico: The Center for American Press, Inc.) 17.

7   George Friedman, *New Orleans: A Geopolitical Prize*, Stratfor, http://22.stratfor.com/news/archive/050903-geopolitics_katrina.php (February 9, 2007).

8   Gulf of Mexico Fact Sheet, Gulf of Mexico — A National Resource, America's Energy Coast, http://www.americasenergycoast.org/pagedetail.php?page_ID=8&detail_ID=60 (September 26, 2008).

9   http://epa.gov/gmpo/about/facts.html

10 http://www.americasenergycoast.org/pagedetail.php?page_ID=8&detail_ID=60

11 http://epa.gov/gmpo/about/facts.html

12 http://epa.gov/gmpo/about/facts.html

13 John Folse, *The Encyclopedia of Cajun and Creole Cuisine* (Gonzales, Louisiana: Chef John D. Folse & Company Publishing, 2004) 5.

14 Peirce F. Lewis, 9.

15 Mississippi River, Wikipedia, the free encyclopedia, http://en.wikipedia.org/wiki/Mississippi_River (March 18, 2009).

16 National Park Service, U.S. Department of the Interior, *Mississippi River Facts*, http://www.nps.gov/miss/riverfacts.htm (March 18, 2009).

17 Port of New Orleans Overview http://www.portno.com/pno_pages/about_overview.htm (March 11, 2009).

18 New Orleans: Economy — Major Industries and Commercial Activity http://www.city-data.com/us-cities/The-South/New-Orleans-Economy.html (September 11, 2008).

19 Port of New Orleans http://www.portno.com/pno_pages/about_overview.htm.

20 Port of New Orleans http://www.portno.com/pno_pages/about_overview.htm.

21 Louisiana Mid-Continent Oil and Gas Association, *Industry Overview*, http://www.lmoga.com/industryoverview.html, (March 18, 2009).

22 Coalition to Restore Coastal Louisiana, *The Issue*, http://www.crcl.org/Issue.html, (March 18, 2009).

23 U.S. Army Corps of Engineers, Bonnet Carrè Spillway Overview, http://www.mvn.usace.army.mil/bcarre/designadvances.asp, (March 25, 2009).

24 Nikki Buskey, "Sea's bounty put south Louisiana on the map," dailycomet.com, (LaFourche Parish, Louisiana), January 29, 2009, http://www.dailycomet.com/article/20090129/LIVING03/901290937?Title=Sea_s_bounty_put_south_Louisiana_on_the_map; Louisiana Seafood Promotion Board, http://www.louisianaseafood.com/, (March 18, 2009)

25   Metairie.com Louisiana, Hurricane Katrina Flooding, http://www.metairie.com/0%20New-Active%20HTML%20&%20Photyo%20Galleries/Hurricane%20Katrina.htm (March 11, 2009).

26   Metairie.com Louisiana, Hurricane Katrina Flooding.

27   John Pope, "Tech College's Growth Noted in Publication," *The Times Picayune*, December 8, 2008 Section B.

28   Elizabeth Mullener, "The Queen of Cuisine," *The Times-Picayune*, October 7, 2007.

29   Stacey Plaisance, "Too many hurricanes threaten bayou way of life in Lafitte," *The Times-Picayune* September 16, 2008.

30   Ivor L. Van Heerden, et al., Team Louisiana, "The Failure of the New Orleans Levee System During Hurricane Katrina," State Project No. 704-92-0022, 20 (2006) Appendix 5: Executive Summary, in James G. Wilkins, et al., *Louisiana Coastal Hazard Mitigation Guidebook*, Louisiana Sea Grant College Program; (Baton Rouge, Louisiana 2008), 193.

31   LaCoast, "Standing Ground Against Advancing Waters Acre by Acre, CWPPRA Projects Beat Back Coastal Demise," *WaterMark*s, December 2008, http://www.lacoast.gov/, (March 19, 2009).

32   Richard Campanella, *Bienville's Dilemma*, (Lafayette: Center for Louisiana Studies, University of Louisiana at Lafayette, 2008), 324.

33   The Earth Institute at Columbia University, Earth Institute News Archive, posted 03/29/07, New Research Analyzes Countries at Greatest Risk from Climate Change Impacts, http://www.earth.columbia.edu/news/2007/story03-29-07.php, (March 9, 2009).

34   Peter Weber, *It Comes Down to the Coasts*, http://www.sdearthtimes.com/et0894/et0894s5.html.

35   Doug Daigle, "Testimony for U.S. Commission on Ocean Policy Gulf of Mexico Regional Meeting (New Orleans, LA) March 8, 2009, http://www. oceancommision.gov/publicomment/gulfcomments/daigle_comment.pdf (March 17, 2009)

36   United Houma Nation, "History Time Line," http://www.unitedhoumanation.org/node/13, (March 23, 2009).

37   Ken Wells, "The Good Pirates of the Forgotten Bayous: Fighting to Save a Way of Life in the Wake of Hurricane Katrina," Louisiana Book Festival (Baton Rouge, LA) October 4, 2008.

38   Barataria-Terrebonne National Estuary Program, *Saving Our Good Earth: A Call to Action*, Barataria-Terrebonne Estuarine System Characterization Report, 1995. (Baton Rouge, Thibodaux).

39   Darran Simon, "Long Goodbye," *The Times-Picayune* September 22, 2008.

40   Gambit Weekly Commentary, September 16, 2008, Vol. 29, Number 38.

41   Joseph Romm, "Typhoon Marys and Cyclone Janes, Why Future Katrinas and Gustavs Will Be Much Worse, part 2, September 3, 2008, http://gristmill. grist.org/story/2008/9/2/145334/3476 (March 17, 2009).

42   U.S. Senate. Hurricane Katrina. "A Nation Still Unprepared." Special Report of the Committee on Homeland Security and Governmental Affairs. S. Rep. No. 109-322 (2006) in Wilkins, et al., 43.

43   FEMA, *Arkansas Severe Storms and Flooding associated with Hurricane Gustav*, Declared September 18, 2008, http://www.fema.gov/news/event. fema?id=10608, (March 27, 2009).

44 Insurance Journal, *Southeast News*, "Too Early to Tell if Kentucky Windstorm will Increase Insurance Rates," September 24, 2008, http://www.insurancejournal. com/news/southeast/2008/09/24/94011.htm, (March 27, 2009).

45 Leslie Williams, "Higher Ground," A study finds that New Orleans has plenty of real estate above sea level that is being underutilized," *The Times-Picayune* April 21, 2007.

46 Leslie Williams, "Higher Ground.

47 Leslie Williams, "Higher Ground.

48 James G. Wilkins, et al., *Louisiana Coastal Hazard Mitigation Guidebook*, Louisiana Sea Grant College Program; (Baton Rouge, Louisiana 2008), 23.

49 *Natural Disasters on the Rise*, The Science and the Environment Bulletin March/April 2003 http://www.ec.gc.ca/Science/sandefeb03/a3_e.html.

50 Chris Rose, "No Direction Known, Getting to YES in the City of NO," *The Oxford Press*, Issue 62, 2008, 90.

51 J.T. Kelley et al., *Living with the Louisiana Shore*, (Durham, NC: Duke University Press 1984), in Wilkins, et al., 1.

52 Bill Reed, "Shifting from 'sustainability' to 'regeneration,' " *Building Research and Information*, Vol. 35, I ssue 6, November 2007, 674-680, online publication www.informaworld.com

53 Lawrence Berkeley, "Climate Change and Wildfire Severity in California," *National Laboratory's Environmental Energy Technologies Division Newsletter*, Winter-Spring 2001-2002, 4, http://eetd.lbl.gov/newsletter/nl9/Climate.html (March 17, 2009).

54 Madeline Vann, "Saving the Wetlands: What Can You Do?" *Natural Awakenings*, S.E. Louisiana Edition, October 2008, 10.

55 Adam Kahane in "The Language of Power and the Language of Love, Solving Tough Problems in Practice," *Shambhala Institute for Authentic Leadership*, Fieldnotes, December 2007.

56 Blog comments on article by Andrew C. Revkin, "*New Orleans: Still Inevitable, and Impossible?*" *Dot Earth*, September 2, 2008, http://dotearth.blogs.nytimes.com/2008/09/02/new-orleans-still-inevitable-and-impossible/, (March 28, 2009).

57 Margaret Swedish, *Living Beyond the "End of the World*," (Maryknoll, NY: Orbis Books, 2008) xxii-xxiii.

58 Peter Weber, *It Comes Down to the Coasts: Part II*, http://www.sdearthtimes.com/et0894/et0894s5.html http://www.sdearthtimes.com/et1094/et1094s7.html (September 22, 2008).

59 Hinrichsen, http://www.peopleandplanet.net/doc.php?id=429&section=6.

60 Hinrichsen, http://www.peopleandplanet.net/doc.php?id=429&section=6.

61 Daigle, http://www.oceancommision.gov/publicomment/gulfcomments/daigle_comment.pdf.

62 Hinrichsen, http://www.peopleandplanet.net/doc.php?id=429&section=6.

63 LaCoast, Watermarks 2008-06 Civic Soldier Battles for the Wetlands — Hope for the Coast Hinges on Awareness, Action, http://www.lacoast.gov/watermarks/2008-06/lawareness_action/index.htm (September 25, 2008).

64 Hinrichsen, http://www.peopleandplanet.net/doc.php?id=429&section=6.

65 John M. Barry, *Rising Tide: The Great Mississippi Flood of 1927 and How It Changed America* (Simon & Schuster 1998) in Wilkins, et al., 50-51.

66   Mark Davis, "Rebuilding coast requires hard choices," *The Times Picayune*, November 29, 2008.

67   Vanessa McKinney, "Sea Level Rise and the Future of the Netherlands," ICE Case Studies, American University, May 2007, http://www.american.edu/ted/ice/dutch-sea.htm (March 16, 2009).

68   Prime Minister Jan Peter Balkenende, "The role of Spain and the Netherlands in Europe," Nueva Economía Fórum (Madrid, Spain) 09-07-2008.

69   Dale Morris, "Dutch Dialogue II," (New Orleans, LA) October 13, 2008.

70   Colin Woodard, "Netherlands Battens Its Ramparts Against Warming Climate" *Christian Science Monitor*, September 4, 2001, reprinted on National Geographic News.com, http://news.nationalgeographic.com/news/2001/08/0829_wiredutch.html (March 16, 2009).

71   Wilkins et al., 2.

72   Campanella, 16.

73   Folse, 50-117.

74   Folse, 246-248.

75   NationMaster.com encyclopedia, http://www.nationmaster.com/encyclopedia/Jazz-funeral (March 11, 2009).

76   Liz Reyes, "Middendorf's Restaurant struggling to reopen after Hurricane Ike," ABC26WGNO, September 20, 2008, http://www.abc26.com/pages/landing/?-Middendorfs-Restaurant-struggling-to-re=1&blockID=63117&feedID=1154 (March 13, 2009).

77   Mark Johnson interview on *Bill Moyers Journal*, October 24, 2008, http://www.pbs.org/moyers/journal/10242008/transcript4.html (March 16, 2009).

78   Gerald Barney, Interview May 2007, in Margaret Swedish, *Living Beyond the "End of the World,"* (Maryknoll, NY: Orbis Books, 2008) 134.

79   Barry Boyce, "Why We Need New Ways of Thinking," *Shambala Sun*, September 2008, 47.

80   Chris Rose, " 'Soul' on Ice," *The Times Picayune*, October 5, 2008, Section D.

81   Kathy Anderson, "Faces of Recovery," *The Times Picayune*, October 5, 2008, Section D.

82   Mark Johnson, http://www.pbs.org/moyers/journal/10242008/transcript4.html.

83   Mark Johnson, http://www.pbs.org/moyers/journal/10242008/transcript4.html.

Related Resources

Advocates for Environmental Human Rights, http://www.whumanrights.org

Barataria-Terrebonne National Estuary Program, http://www.btnep.org/home.asp

Bayou Rebirth Wetlands Restoration and Education, http://www.bayourebirth.org/source/shtml/home.shtml

Coalition to Restore Coastal Louisiana, http://www.crcl.org/

Deep South Center for Environmental Justice, http://www.dscej.org

Ecological Footprint Quiz, http://www.myfootprint.org, www.kidsfootprint.org

Friends of New Orleans, http://www.friendsofneworleans.org/help/index.php#advocate

Gulf of Mexico Foundation, http://www.gulfmex.org

Gulf Restoration Network, http://healthygulf.org

Lake Pontchartrain Basin Foundation, http://www.saveourlake.org/wetlands.htm

Louisiana Sea Grant Law and Policy Program, http://www.lsu.edu/sglegal

Make It Right, http://www.makeitrightnola.org

Make New Orleans Home, http://www.makeneworleanshome.com/about/geography.html

MoveOn. Org, http://pol.moveon.org/event/events/index.html?action_id=164

NOLA Environmental Compliance Databank, http://www.nolaenvironmental.gov

People and Planet, http://www.peopleandplanet.net

Scorcard.org (provides specific data on pollution in your zip code and tools to take action), http://www.scorecard.org

Teaching Tolerance, U.S. Map of Social Justice, Louisiana http://www.tolerance.org/maps/social_justice/state.jsp?state_id=19

The Coast Guardians, http://www.americasenergycoast.org/page.php?page_ID=8

The New Orleans Convention and Vistors Bureau, http://www.neworleanscvb.com/static/index.cfm/contentID/732/sectionID/1/subsectionID/732

Turtle Cove Environmental Research Center, http://www.selu.edu/acad_research/programs/turtle_cove/index.html

Voice of the Wetlands, http://www.voiceofthewetlands.org

Volunteer Louisiana, http://www.volunteerlouisiana.gov/1800Vol/OpenIndexAction.do

We can solve the climate crisis, http://www.wecansolveit.org

Index

Your Pages

(as explained on page 73)